The Rising and Falling of the Sun and Moon

GW00496559

Leia Lous

Note...

I've written a poetry book, its filled with my secrets, my emotions, my life story so far, it's a confession I suppose. I finished writing it in October 2022, it was then March 2023, and I still hadn't released it yet. I guess I was a little afraid of what people will think when they read them, or what they will think of me. Maybe they didn't know about things I have written about, or wouldn't expect it, maybe they knew but are disappointed in me or think I should feel ashamed, think that I am just an emotional teenage girl. But then I really sat down and looked at what I created, all by myself, the time it took, the strength it took, the story it tells, the feelings that need to be heard, the sweat, blood and tears that went into it. Then it hit me, who cares? Who cares what anyone else thinks? I deserve to feel proud of myself, I turned such a dark and sad chapter of my life and I'm sure many others have experienced the same, into something beautiful, comforting and creative. Maybe it is my confession, but perhaps for some other people it can be their comfort, the realisation that they are far from alone in the way they feel. I must do this for me, and hope that many other people will read it and relate to it in their own different ways, my dream would be that it helps them to get through anything life throws your way.

So here it is! I am so grateful that I can say it and truly mean it, I am proud of myself, so please read and allow yourself to think and feel whatever it is that floods to your mind as your read.

My last message to you... you are not alone.

Leia Lous

My counsellor would tell me,
That to recover and to heal,
First, I must acknowledge and accept
The way that I am feeling.
So many times,
At the latest hours of night,
I sit with pen and paper,
and I write poems.
As I spill out the words I cannot say,
That's when it hits me,
I'm writing about it,
which means its hurts,
Which means it means something,
Which means its stuck in my head,
Which means I'm thinking about it,
Which means I care,
Which means this is how I am feeling.
I told my counsellor,
I dismiss my feelings,
Deny them to anyone who asks.
Yet my notebook knows everything,
I can't hide away from the ink-stained paper,
It knows me inside out.
I told her that I hate myself
For being so Incapable of talking
To real people who can respond.
She smiled,
And told me to write, and write,
And write some more.
So, I suppose this book is a confession.
This book is the truth,
And this book took
all my strength,
My sadness, heartbreak, grief, anger,
But it also reminds you and me,
Of my recovery, growth, love, happiness.
You must fall to rise,
You must lose to win,
You must feel to understand.
Things do get better,
She promised me that,
Now I am promising you.

~ From someone who knows what it's like to feel alone...
you are not alone.

For

Joanne, Carol, and Melanie.
Three special women
who supported me through everything,
there for me no matter what,
and never failed to make me
Smile.

I love you to the moon and back.
You are my sunshine.

The falling
~ sadness ... 7-24
~ heartbreak ... 25-44
~ grief ... 45-61
~ anger ... 62-78

The rising
~ recovery ... 80-97
~ growth ... 98-113
~ love ... 114-129
~ happiness ... 130-147

The Falling.

sadness.

If you crack a glow stick, it turns into a beautiful flow of colour and luminous light that catches the retina, the focus of your ability to see, and your brain bursts with feelings of transcendence, admiration, awe and fascination.

Like a ray of sunshine.

But crack it too hard for too long, it breaks, the kaleidoscope of happy visions fades away, dies, the sparkle loses its grip and gradually leaves the body, the glow stick.

Similar to the likes of a person's spark, passion, energy. You can watch them grow, change, blossom, burst with their own colours and enlightenment, but you push them, drag, pull, damage them too much for one beating heart to handle, they break.

They fade until their glow stick of a soul is no more.

Just like dreams do not force it to happen, if you can't crack the glow stick without it breaking, it's more than okay to get some help, the glow stick may not have the strength to flourish by themselves.

If it refuses to flourish no matter what, it might be defective. Its light, it shine, its beauty may have faded away a long time ago, but you would never have realised as a glow stick holds the same shape no matter how hard it is snapped, pulled, twisted.

It's an actor, a deception.

If the light can no longer shine, like a person may despise the bearing of a smile, sometimes glow sticks need to be thrown away and you must let them go.

~if you crack a glowstick

The fall,
You would think that is what would
petrify you the most,
paralyse your body to the bone,
play on your mind like a magic trick,
but the concept of standing on your own two feet
became a worser feeling than robbing those
muscles and bones of their exhausting duty,
when you mind had been the only captain of the sinking ship,
also known as your heart,
for longer than a sailor could voyage across
the Pacific Ocean.

~The Fall

I felt the absence of love in my head, and in my heart.
But not in my eyes, my hands, my ears, nor my body.
It stuck to me like a leech sucking me dry.

I saw the smiles and laughs from those I adore,
But I hadn't the strength to join.
I heard the words of another claiming they love,
But I could not feel their meaning.
I felt the hands wrap around my motionless body,
But I still ached from head to toe.

They want to help,
They want to understand,
They want to help.

But my only need is to be left alone,
Tell my friends I love them, and I'll miss them,
But I am not sorry.
Tell my family I love them, and I'll miss them,
But I am not sorry.
Tell my future and whatever it might or might not have brought,
Maybe I should be sorry,
But I am not sorry.

Sorry.
Sorry, it's too late, you can't save me now.
Sorry, that I see no way out,
But down.
down.

~I'm sorry because I'm not sorry

Leia Lous

What happens when the darkness you've been locking up inside, decides to make a home of its bars?

You've swallowed the agonising lump hanging in the back of your throat with no hope of regurgitating that pain.

It lives inside of you, the black, the shadows, the darkness, and it paints your heart all over in despair, until it matches the emotions screaming through your tired, dreary eyes.

Your aching brain acts as a pool for the thoughts and memories that were once alive, to drown in.

You scream, cry, throw up as you watch the light blue water turn to a deep murky red as the blood in your body becomes the final thing to give up on you, it floods out in waves.

I learnt that it's never the darkness that you should be most afraid of, it's what lurks within, and when those shadows attack, they eat you alive. Your soul becomes nothing more than a final tear drop, and the motionless body without a beating heart to carry…

falls heavily to the bathroom floor.

~where the darkness lives

Leia Lous

Depression is bittersweet,
You crave nothing but comfort in the darkness.
You search for that feeing in anything and everything,
After all,
There is no visible stream of light in the dark,
Only what lurks within.
But darkness only breeds more darkness,
So, what can you do?
But surrender to the shadows,
Embrace them with open arms,
For all you need is-
Comfort.
In the darkness.

~depression is bitterswee

In times like this
When I first wake up
When my eyes begin to roll
My body begs not to get up.

The sun falls to the ground
and rolls swiftly away
Flowers cry and behead themselves
They all know it's a Monday.

The birds stop their singing
The grass wont dance in the breeze
The bees give up on their giggles
I hear the wind whispering please.

I barely feel like living
But all that's left alive here is me
I wish to see a rainbow for colours breed life
But the raindrops and the sunshine both laugh at me.

We have all been dying
All that's below the blanket of sky
But we forgot to enjoy the view
Mother Nature questions why?

~to wake up is to live

Leia Lous

I have always loved
When the flowers bloom boldly,
and the birds sing softly,
Adored the shower of sunlight,
and the clouds that float by.
I have always loved the leaves,
The way they dance gently in a breeze,
and that soft whispering sound the wind makes,
like even nature wakes up and lives.
Yet that draining feeling that visits
Once in a while,
Consumes me like a veil over my soul.
As I admire the petals and the branches that sway beside me,
Watching the beautiful birds dive in freedom,
And the giggling of bees, breathing of fish,
there seems to only be sorrow and envy
where there should be joy.
It settles on my skin like November rain,
enough to freeze what was once warm within.
At any other time, I would have called for help,
asked politely for the warmth of the rays of sun,
The nudge from the wind to keep moving,
The strength I needed to ward it off.
I no longer ask from help from those
Who provide for everyone with everything they have.
I don't deserve that kind of attention, I'll manage.
Now I just let it sink in, drop by drop,
I feel like it's built up and built up until there's
A whole ocean falling upon my shoulders instead of rain,
All the sadness I have carried forever,
has transformed into a cloud large enough
to block the sun.
They say it can't rain forever,
That at some point it must come to an end,
that the last raindrop would have fallen,
And the sun will visit once again.

...

Leia Lous   14

...

That doesn't seem to matter to me now,
I've become immune to the sun, the cloud, the rain.
All of it seems the same, another day, same old things.
I'll let the flowers bloom for me, birds sing for me,
Sunlight screams for me, clouds fly for me,
Leaves dance for me, wind talk for me,
Birds be free for me, bees giggle for me.
Fish can breathe, for I no longer can.
Maybe that's selfish,
But I'll stay here comfortably numb,
Come rain or shine, it doesn't matter.

~come rain or shine

Leia Lous

I am lonely in places
I was unaware even existed
Within my body, my heart, my soul.
Within me.
I'm exhausted by strength so much,
That I long for an arm to hold me up,
No one holds me, I am alone.
I'm weak from simply walking so much,
That I crave someone to move my feet forward,
No one walks for me, I am alone.
I'm tired of talking so much,
That I wish someone could read my mind,
No one can hear me, I am alone.
I'm drained from overthinking so much,
That I need someone to climb into my brain
And reorganise everything for me to
Make sense of,
No one could understand me, I am alone.
From the outside looking in,
It's incredibly difficult to understand.
From the inside looking out,
It's even more so to explain.

~lonely in place.

I thought mirrors were supposed to tell you the truth,
Somewhere between the lies,
I turned into nothing but a reflection-
I didn't recognise.

I used to shine so brightly,
That the sun would scream in jealousy.
I used to laugh so contagiously,
That even the bees would giggle in the breeze.
I used to blossom so beautifully,
That the flowers would pick their petals in envy.
I used to live so freely,
That the gushes of wind surrendered to my force.

But now the ground has destructed beneath my feet,
And I've fallen heavily into a dark hole.
Deeper.
deeper.
deeper.
I am so down that-

I am so painted with darkness,
That the sun laughs mockingly at me.
I am so wet with tears streaming down my cheeks,
That the rain refuses to offer any support.
I am so dead inside, outside,
That the flowers show off their freshly grown petals.
I am so trapped in a hole with no escape,
The mirror of truth, between the lies,
And the reflection I didn't recognise-

Was me, in the depths of the dirt,
and the ground where nothing lived.

~mirrors in the dirt

Leia Lous

17

You can pretend it's not there,
Until you are sitting on the floor of the shower,
The tears bawling from my sore eyes
Make you wetter than the drop falling from above.
Your wrists stinging, throbbing so badly,
That it somehow feels good, comforting.

You can pretend it's not there,
Until your legs just want to surrender to the pain,
Fall heavily to the ground, wherever you may be,
And fold up like origami hiding from the world.
Your motionless body, without any energy,
Shuts down to die, relaxing.

You can pretend it's not there,
Until you feel a knife plunge into your stomach,
After every little lie you tell your loved ones,
I'm fine. I'm okay. I'm just tired.
Your heart is aching to spill the truth, but your heart
Tells you no one wants to know, thinking.

It's as if,
That cold shoulder-
Will forever feel warm to her.

~comfort in a cold shoulde

People don't understand me
When I say I want to hurt myself.
As if pain can only result to
Agony, crying, screaming, dying.
I do cry.
Sometimes I scream.
But sometimes that is the
Best feeling,
Because for those sharp ten minutes,
I am feeling
something.
Which is more than I can say
For every day, hour, minute,
That I am not hurting myself.
I feel nothing but numbness.
emptiness.
No pain or agony could be worse,
That the pain and agony
of feeling nothing at all.
So, next time you ask me
Why would you do that to yourself?
Remember,
You can't see my pain or agony,
Because through your eyes it's not there.
But my heart has been bleeding forever,
To feel pain to me,
Is to feel anything at all.
Handle me with care.

~fragile

Leia Lous

It's only a scratch,
Until it's a cut.
"What's the mark?"
"It was the dog."
It's only a lie
Never the truth.
It's only a cut,
Until it's a wound.
"What's with the plaster?"
"Dropped the straighteners."
It's only a lie.
Never the truth.
It's only a wound,
Until it's a scar.
"Why did you never tell me?"
"You were never there to tell."
That's the truth.
Your sympathy is a lie.

~only a scrat

The three phases of a dandelion,
Represent the sun, moon and stars.
The blossomed yellow flower,
The sun.
The white puff ball,
The moon.
The dispersing seeds,
The stars.

But I see a dandelion,
And I see me.

A dandelion grows and flourishes,
Its sun the colours of yellow and orange.
Then the moon of a dandelion builds up,
And it spreads itself all over like stars in the sky,
Until all the dull and lifeless patches of dirt
Have a chance to grow into something
Beautiful
And
Strong.

I grew and I flourished,
As did my heart,
And I spread myself all over.
I gave parts of myself,
Like happiness, love, pride, confidence,
I gave them to people
Who claimed to need it more than I did.

But then I was left,
With a fragile and weak stem
A living thing robbed of its beauty.
Yet no one stole that beauty,
The dandelion just had too good a heart,
And chose to help the other living things,
And forgot to live herself.

~dandelions grow in my veins

Leia Lous

21

I used to hate sleeping,
Petrified of the idea that I'd be
Alone with my thoughts,
That they could swallow me whole,
For I would be unable to see
The form of a monster they take in
The darkness.
I used to hate going to bed but
Now it seems to be the thing I crave
Every minute throughout the day.
I wish for nothing but the peace and quiet,
The silence in the loneliness,
For the sound of nothing and I
Have become quite good friends.
Most of all, I wish to escape.
Sometimes, I count the minutes
That I lay there empty, drifting away,
So that I can acknowledge how little I am feeling.
In the darkness I somehow feel
That all the weight of the world
Has been lifted from my shoulders,
And freed me.
Yet, it never seemed to occur to me,
Until it became a little too late,
That it was not setting me free,
It was hiding me, trapping me,
I was restricted and contained
In my own bed.
For I would never leave it,
The silence hypnotised me,
In a trance I was tricked into believing
Emptiness was the answer to my troubles.
If I felt nothing, nothing could hurt me.
But if nothing hurt me, nothing could change me,
Nothing could help me grow,
Nothing could help fix me.
If I felt nothing, I couldn't feel happiness,
Nor love either.

...

Leia Lous

...
I fell so deeply into its curse that
I was tied up, held down, pinned,
To my bed, I could no longer move.
In the end,
The silence engulfed me,
The darkness swallowed me,
My thoughts ate me alive,
There was nothing left of me,
But a puddle of tears on my pillow.

~Friends with the silence

So much sadness has come at once,
That it almost feels like no sadness has come at all.

I have been trapped in a hole for so long,
That I seem to have made myself comfortable.

So many thoughts and feelings live rent free in my head,
That they seem to have built their own home up there.

When everything is draining,
Is there really anything left to drain?

What I am trying to say is-

How can you pile depression on top of other depression,
And expect it to look any different?

Emptiness means absolutely nothing,
If you stare at it
Long enough.

~why has the uncomfortable become comfortable

Leia Lous

heartbreak.

Heartbreak.
Seems so simple
When you think about it.
Even the word is just
Black and white.
Heart.
break.
For the first time
It was clear to me
What I was feeling,
My heart
stopped.
It broke.
And it's funny,
Because in my head
I'm full of fog and mist
That I can't find
My way through,
But with you and me
It's a clear pathway
I can see straight.
I know what I feel,
You broke me,
And God it was painful.
I cried, I sobbed, I screamed.
Begging to super glue
The pieces of my shattered heart
Back together,
Me and you,
Back together.
But I lay here with the fragments
Of my broken heart,
And I realise
I'm now alone,
And only I can put those pieces
Back together.
Me.

...

Leia Lous

...
Seems so simple
When you think about it.
Because at the end of the day,
The black and white,
Is that I am the only one
Who has stayed with me since day one
And never left.
My heart is mine,
What kind of person would I be?
To leave that gift of life and love
Inside my body,
To remain broken.

~A simple diagnosis

I wish I could say that
as a person who writes
words down everyday
As a way of processing,
recovering, healing,
That I am good with words.
But that is far from the truth.
A pen and paper is so easy,
My voice and your ears,
That is something
completely different.
I could write for days
About all I feel for you,
I could speak no longer
than a few seconds,
When you look at me,
When you touch me,
When you truly see me,
It's like I'm naked,
Not the lack of clothes,
But completely transparent,
you witness every part of me,
Every thought and feeling,
Like its painted across my forehead.
I can't speak because I can't breathe,
So much of me is built on fear,
Scared that perhaps love is something
Forever far from my reach,
Not belonging to a heart like mine.
You see, love,
Love is a silent emotion that
in time becomes part of the oxygen
you will need to breathe,
and I get so unsure that it's there,
So petrified I will lose it,
Any form of removal and
My emotions begin to choke,
My heart begins to choke,
I begin to choke,
And my voice hides away.

...

Leia Lous

...

So, I get a pen, and paper,
And I write those three
dangerous yet beautiful words
In the form of poetry
For me and me only to read
Until I can feel something.
Then I wonder,
Why don't I hear those words,
Only read them in my own ink?
You breathe, I choke.
You don't care, I write poetry.
You don't say it because you don't mean it,
I write I love you because I already know
That you don't, won't, never did, never will
Love me.

~You breathe, I choke.

They told me I shine as bright as the sun,
They told me my light could never be undone,
They told me my spark was one that stunned,
They never told me about the dark.

I thought if you shine, they will notice,
I thought my light breeds hypnosis,
I thought love was a diagnosis,
They never told me about the dark.

I wish I knew that the shine wasn't for him,
I wish I knew my light must sometimes dim,
I wish I knew the spark wasn't beneath the skin.
They should have told me about the dark.

He told me I shine as bright as the sun at its peak,
His skin was pale and to him my light was weak.
He told me still that my spark was so unique,
His skin was pale, and I realised-
It was the darkness that made him feel alive.

We were like the sun and the moon,
We share the sky and all its beauty and soon
We would meet each other in passing just after noon,
but we could never shine at the same time together.
After all, every day starts then ends with
The sun and the moon.

~The sun and the moon

There was a girl.
Yeah, I hate to admit,
But that girl was me.
She thought that if she
Never gave her heart away,
That it'd never end up broken.

But this girl,
God forbid her ever showing
That she could be scared.
Hidden beneath her skin
She feared love like it could kill her,
Though it was no match to her fear
of being alone.

Love was so unfamiliar,
So distant from a soul like hers.
She gave all the love she knew
To everyone and everything,
But received nothing in return.
It was as if something
She'd known since birth
Forever saw her as a stranger.

So, she kept her heart to herself,
Petrified that in the hands of another
It would shatter or crumble.
Until she met him.
She thought she'd found her world,
But then the world found out
Just how vulnerable beneath the skin
How fragile her earth really was.

And so, he stormed.
He earth quaked.
He shook her earth,
Right down to its core.
My ground was taken from me,
And my heart buried in its remains.

~In the remains of her earth

Leia Lous

I wanted to write down
Everything I felt for you,
Everything I thought about you,
Everything I loved about you,
And everything I hated about you,
Now that there is no longer
A you and me,
But somehow my page remained blank,
No words, no scribbles, nothing.
But in all honesty,
I could not have described it
Any better than that,
A blank page
At the back of a story
Never meant to be written.

~Blank pag

If I told you about the darkness
That lives inside of me,
Would you still look at me
Like I am the sun?

If I told you that this darkness
Has flooded into my heart,
Would you still love me like
My heart is made of gold?

If I told you my heart is
Now black and blue,
Would you still paint it
With colours of love?

If I told you I loved you
But my heart is filled with pain,
Would you say it back and mean it
Or feed it with more aching
And make my heartache your gain?

~Would you?

Leia Lous

If my heart was made of glass,
It would have shattered long ago.

If my heart was made of grass,
You would've unravelled me like so,

You'd take my love
With all my kindness,
You'd take me apart piece by piece,
With violence so mindless.

If I knew when I'd met you,
You'd leave me with nothing left,
I'd build my heart from sticks and stones,
To shield me from your theft.

You took my good will for a weakness
And treated me how you liked,
You didn't only break my heart,

It was my happiness that you swiped.

~Thief

Leia Lous

In the end,
my fear of losing them,
was no match to my
fear of loving them.
The overwhelming horror,
Of losing a diamond in the ocean,
Of smashing a jewel into thousands,
Of chipping a gem at its core,
Of damaging the power of a crystal.
Our love was expensive,
I gave you every penny I had,
For you to make a profit by
Investing in someone more worthy.
I became nothing but a rock to you.
I always dreamt of being loved like gold,
but I settled for someone
who loved me like silver,
and you wonder why I tarnished.
When is it that you realise,
Real, honest, true love,
It has no price,
Only two hearts
That find treasure in the arms
Of each other.

~My heart at your expense

Leia Lous

I'd say that you broke my heart,
But much more of me is now broken,
Like my heart was a glass bottle
You smashed on a wall.
Let's say I was built like a glass bottle,
You were the hydration that filled me
From my head to my toes.
But little by little, you took sips, gulps,
swallowed what was left swimming within me.
One sip, you go ahead and lie to me,
If you want to pour it all out now
that's fine with me, I feel much less.
A gulp, you get bored like you always do,
If you want to try a new flavour,
that's fine with me, just promise
you'll let me go before you do.
Swallow, you continue to hurt me,
If you want to shatter all of me now,
That's fine with me, I won't feel anything.
If I'm not good enough for you, honestly,
I'd rather be swimming in an empty pool,
Than drowning in your ocean of poison.
I'd rather have been a glass half empty,
Than a glass half full of you.
You that intoxicates me,
From my head to my toes.

~*Glass bottle*

Leia Lous   36

Tell me why,
You broke me.
Tell me why,
I wasn't good enough.
Tell me why,
You needed more.
Tell me why,
She was better.
Tell me why,
I deserved any of this.
Tell me why,
You don't even care.
Tell me why,
You don't hurt like I do.
Tell me why,
You can laugh at me.
Tell me why,
You don't have a heart.
Tell me why,
I blame myself.
Tell me why,
Why me?
Why me and you?
Why you and her?
Why? Why? Why?
I was so confused,
because I needed to
gain greater perspective,
to take a step back
and see the wide-angle version.
There was a lot more to see,
little wonder I couldn't
figure things out back then.
I'll tell you why.
You didn't break me,
I can fix myself.

...

Leia Lous

...

I was more than good enough,
You needed less than me.
She wasn't better,
She was just the easier option.
I didn't deserve any of this,
But ill grow every day from it.
Maybe you don't care,
But one day you will.
No, you won't hurt like I do,
Because you can't love like I do.
Who cares if you're laughing at me,
Jokes on you.
You do have a heart,
A weak, fragile, insecure one.
I did blame myself,
Yet the only thing I ever did wrong
Was to fall in love with you.
That's why.
That's why heartbreak is temporary,
Hearts are built to be broken,
Because you have choices,
Someone else can come along
And glue the pieces back together,
Or you can realise the strength you hold,
And breathe something new, fresh,
And so incredibly beautiful
From its remains.

~why, why, wh

Leia Lous

Driving in the rain is like flirting with death,
There's a strange comfort in it.
Yet it was never the driving nor the rain
That attracted the danger, nor the comfort.

It was the body in the driver's seat,
The beating heart that seemed to
pulsate fear through my veins,
Just by a single touch.
The piercing eyes that seemed to
Look directly into my soul,
Reading all the hidden thoughts in my mind,
Like I was an open book.
The mouth I seemed to
imagine ripping through my flesh,
And swallowing me whole.

It was the body in the driver's seat,
The soft gentle voice
That calmed all my nerves,
With just one whisper.
The strong hands that
Held onto me when id fall,
Like they gave me the strength to stand.
The comforting words of
'I really do love you'
Like they'd paint my heart in gold.

The comfort of the thought of you,
But the danger of the truth of you.
Love is a quiet emotion that in time
becomes part of the oxygen you need
to simply breathe,
and so, though you may feel
Unsure that it's truly there,
any form of removal and
the emotions begin to choke.

...

...
You suffocate me with love.
I can't breathe when I'm around you.
You play trick or treat with my heart,
Until the treats became a manipulation
Into believing you never tricked me
In the first place.

Driving in rain is like flirting with death,
But loving you was death flirting with me.
My heart will die by the time
We reach the end of the road.

~flirting with death

I suppose I should apologise,
That I took it upon myself to build
A home out of you,
Like you were made of clay.
I moulded you with my own hands
Into something only I needed,
I put bricks onto your shoulders,
Never realising the weight you would carry.
I cemented my heart so that it would
Be placed directly next to yours.
I drilled all the pain of my past
Screwed it deep into your mind,
The agony you felt made out to be all my fault.
For I took it upon myself to build
A home out of you,
I didn't realise you had
No intention
Of inviting me to stay.

~A home out of you

The difference between you and me,
Among all the happiness,
All the memories,
All the laughing,
All the crying,
All the plans for the future,
A future that never belonged to
Me
And
You.

Was that,
All that you really wanted was
To be intimate
With a body.
All that I really wanted was
To be intimate
With a heart.

Funny how one word,
No-

Can break an actor
From deceiving the one who loves them,
Because all they want is
Yes.
And all you said was
No.

You made me feel foolish,
That an object,
As you see me,
Could refuse a machine like
You.

~My legs do not open for a machine

I should be so angry,
Everyone tells me.
I should be shouting,
Everyone tells me.
I should be crying,
Everyone tells me.
I should be kicking and punching,
Everyone tells me.

I wish I could be angry,
I wish I could cry,
And shout and punch and kick,
I wish I could tell you that
I hate you
And you broke
my heart.

But everyone needs to stop
Telling me.
They don't know.
What loving you was like.
I cannot do those things
They tell me to do,
Because I was in love
With you.
I said that love would never end,
To hate you would make me a
Liar.
I am not a liar,
I am not like you.
I was just a girl in love.

~Liar, Liar, my hearts on fire

Leia Lous

Tonight,
I lit three candles.
One for you,
I blew that one out.
One for me,
And I watched
the flame get bigger.
And one for
Us.
The candle
Glowed,
And flickered,
And warmed
My heart and soul,
And then it
burnt out.
It lasted a while,
And in that time
I reminisced
All the good memories
Of us,
And how warm and bright
You
Made
Me
Feel.
But just like the candle
We burnt out and died.
There was nothing left
Of the candle to burn.
But it was worth it,
And I'm so grateful of
The few minutes
Of peace it brought to
My life.

~A burnt out cand

Leia Lous

grief.

Some measure time by minutes and hours, others by the rising and falling of the sun. how can one measure anything if every time they smiled the world would stop spinning?

It's like when there's a daisy that grows from an errant crack in the dried and aged concrete, a tiny, yet captivating splash of colour that transforms the wide scenery and draining atmosphere with its simplistic perfection. That's what her smile was like.

Like a breath of fresh air, like the sun as it rises from the distant horizon and reflects off the dainty shells resting and sleeping gently on the shore. Their presence became a beacon of light to shine upon my cloudy skies, my worst days. Like a ray of sunshine.

When they are not around, it rains, it pours, it thunders. Yet rain was always our favourite because we were too broken and numb to cry, so the sky did it for us. The two of us would lay there, anywhere, cause the feeling of the sharp, biting, wet drops running down our cheeks as it floods from the clouds above us, was just enough to make us feel a little more alive.

Sometimes we would sink into that moment long enough to see the darkness wash over and the petite shimmers of hope would appear, well, once upon a time when I held on to hope. Maybe one day the rain will feel the same against my motionless body as it did yesterday and all the days before, and the stars will glisten the same way they did when they swam in the mirrors of your eyes.

You always said you loved the stars, in fact I grew to love them too, funny how they seem to shine brighter now that you have joined them... and with that, there was no more rain, no more thunder, no more five minutes prior.

Just me, myself, and the downpour.

~swimming stars and dancing rain

Leia Lous   46

Grief is a dark cloud
That lurks above me,
Its thunder holds me captive,
The rainfall weighing me down
With memories of how it used to be,
Each moment now passed with the wind,
Each raindrop matching the timing of my tears,
Drenching me from head to toe in thoughts of you.
Now I sit and wonder,
When will this cloud blow over?
When will I finally meet skies of blue?
For you were the clear, without you its foggy.
Though you lay at rest, at peace and grounded,
But to the living above you the pain overwhelms
Those who are now left behind.
A whole universe of memories is all we have left
To meet with you once again,
Though we can no longer feel your touch,
Or hear your voice or see your face.
A sense of never-ending loneliness
Walks beside grief hand in hand.

~Drenched in thoughts of you

The thing about experiencing grief is that
It's not the ending of life that will haunt you,
But the space in which that life had thrived,
Now left empty and cold through and through.
The things that are now gone forever,
With one final wave goodbye,
A feeling that a piece of you is nowhere to be found,
Now that they are flying up high.
Like a book with pages that have been lost,
Forgetting things that you know was once there,
A question without an answer,
Within the denial there comes despair.
A song stopped halfway through,
A life that you took for granted,
For you were not prepared to lose them,
Yet a guilt in you has been planted.
For you forgot to enjoy the little things in life,
Yet now you look back and realise
That, they were the big things in life,
For they made you feel the most alive.

~*Little things, big thing*

Leia Lous

Sometimes,
when I think I've accepted
that you are no longer here,
they start playing that song.
The lyrics pull the strings
of my wounded heart.
The beat shoots bullets
into my stomach full of
dead butterflies.
The rhythm spins
my head into circles
until I can longer see straight.
I can't help but to think about
Me and You.
I really believed that
I was done with the hardest part,
when you were no longer
wrapped in my arms.
I wish I knew that was only
the start.
The song ends,
The emptiness hasn't.

~ 'Cry to me' Solomon Burke

Leia Lous

It has been quite some years,
But this feeling, it still hasn't passed,
I never imagined for this long it would last,
I try so hard to move on,
Where my head is at, I can't keep track,
I try to escape the pain and emptiness
yet it keeps crawling straight back.
I miss you so much now my heart is so sore,
As time passes swiftly by, I miss you even more,
Your reassuring smile and loving face,
I want nothing more than for you to know
That no one could ever take
your place,
For here in my head and my heart
Is where you will always belong,
Whether you are here or not
In my ears ill always hear your song.

~Your so

Leia Lous

I thought I heard your voice in the wind today,
And strangely I turned around to meet your face,
The warmth from the wind blow comforted me,
But you were not there to embrace.
I thought I could feel your touch in the sun today,
As its warming light flooded the sky,
I shut my eyes hoping if I blinked, you'd be there,
But they opened and you were still flying high.
I thought I saw your eyes in a puddle,
Staring at the reflection as I watched the falling rain,
Although it seemed as each raindrop fell,
The drops on the floor spelt your name.
I thought I should hold you close to my heart today,
For when with you I used to feel complete,
You may have died but you are not gone,
For you always live inside of me.

~Live inside of me

Leia Lous

Grief has a way of isolating you
from the rest of the living world,
and it takes an unimaginable strength
to reconnect and weave yourself anew
into the fabric of living,
to give yourself a chance of happiness,
A future without them at first feels like
A punishment only breeds pain and misery.
For you have lost who makes life worth living,
All that runs erratically around your head,
Are questions, what's the point?
Why them and not me?
Why should I live without them?
What is life now I have lost my reason to live?
The agonising truth is that
No one will last forever,
Well, perhaps not physically,
But life goes on and time moves forward,
As shall you learn to live without those you lost,
But they are not gone,
They will never be forgotten,
As long as they remain smiling,
Laughing, dancing, singing, breathing,
In the back of your mind,
And the bottom of your heart.

~Remain living

Leia Lous

They say you should cherish memories,
And believe me I do that too,
But what if I don't want memories,
I just want to cherish you.

But I can't keep you in a treasure chest,
Though a diamond you are,
I can no longer see your face,
But I reach for you in a star.

If my tears could build a staircase,
From down here to the sky,
Id float on a cloud,
Laugh and smile as you fly.

If love could have saved you,
You never would have died,
Because ill love you forever,
At least I know,
That you really
tried.

~you were a diamond

Grief has no end to it,
but it will consistently change,
it's a pathway rather than a place to stay,
Grief is the turning of a page.
But it's hard to turn the page when you know
someone will not return in the next chapter,
but the story just goes on,
Same as the memories we capture.
Grief is not a sign of weakness,
but it becomes the price of love,
For the sky cannot return,
Who now takes form as a star above.
The sky looks so very different
when you have someone you love up there,
Their absence is like the sky,
it spreads over everything,
But leaves your heart bare.

~Their absence is like the sky

Leia Lous

If the process of grief had a script,
I would recite every single line,
For now, I am helplessly confused,
Ever since you have left me behind.
I have learnt I am a brilliant actor,
A master of deception,
For every day I say I'm fine without you,
Yet I've lost all sense of direction.
So, yes, if grief had a script,
At least I would know what to say and do,
Maybe I would learn how to live without you,
If I make it to the end of act two.
Grief is the last act of love
we must give to those we have lost,
For where there is deep grief there was great love,
Grief is loving hards final cost.
I have not heard your voice in years,
but my heart has conversations with you every day,
Maybe death has its very own script,
For I can imagine exactly what you'd say.
Goodbyes hurt when the story is not finished,
and the book has been closed
before it had the chance to truly begin,
But those few pages will never be disposed,
Those memories will forever live within.

~If grief had a script

Leia Lous

I wish I could replace this goodbye,
With a 'see you later',
Or 'see you soon',
'I'll see you in a bit',
'Don't worry'.
But this goodbye isn't temporary.
I won't see you tomorrow,
Or the next day,
Or next week,
Or next month,
or next year.
People always say to me,
With fake sympathy,
And superficial bouquets
Of pity flowers,
'You will see them again one day'.
When, I ask.
When will I see them again.
The closest I can get to them,
Is through my dreams,
Of which pull tears from my eyes.
I can't touch them,
I can't hear them,
I can't feel them,
I can't hug them,
I can't tell them
How much I love them,
And I can't tell them 'goodbye'.
Instead, I said 'see you later',
But later didn't exist.
Later follows me around
as I desperately wait
To see you again,
And replace 'see you later'
With 'goodbye' instead,
So I don't have this overwhelming guilt,
That we made each other think
We would see each other again.
But now your gone,
Without the goodbye you deserved.

~ 'See you late

I lay awake in the night,
Or am I just blind to the light,
For I no longer see the day,
Now that you have flown away.
In every breath I regret,
I only sleep to forget,
That I never said goodbye,
Before you were gifted to the sky.
I wish I could see your face once more,
And hug you tighter than before,
I wish we could have one more day together,
Though our memories will last forever.
So, although I couldn't say those words,
I hope you hear them from a little bird,
As I whisper to you in the wind,
This is goodbye to you,
An angel you have always been.

~Goodbye

Leia Lous

Let this feeling of grief
flow through you like a river
in the mountains passes
it will disintegrate and create new channels,
yet the new drift could become
Stronger than it ever was before.
And this new process,
is time as the rivers and lakes tell it,
not in the same language as the clocks.
It is time that stretches unmeasured
For rivers will continue to ripple,
And time will always move along,
The loss will last forever,
But the grief will come to an end,
For acceptance is the new channel
You can swim your way through,
If you build up the strength
To climb a mountain.

~Rivers of grie

It's ironic really,
How once we start to feel better,
We also often feel deep sadness,
Grieving all that we missed out on,
Whilst we lived in the darkness.
It starts to punch us in the face,
How much has changed in the dark,
How many people bailed on us in the dark,
How people's opinions shifted while in the dark,
What the young us actually deserved.
Little me deserved to grow up in light,
In sunshine, for she was known as
Little miss sunshine.
Now, ironically,
It feels like that sunlight has betrayed me,
I spent so long staring into the shadows
Of whom I used to be,
That the new-born light reflecting off her,
Blinds me with the truth.
Little me has gone, walked away, given up.
She captured the sun in her soft palms,
And watched it melt away through her fingers.
I tried to drink it like a potion,
But no medicine can cure grief,
No drug can bring back the me, that's now dead.

~Little me

I don't know if I blinked at the wrong moment,
Or the lights flickered and stole my vision,
Or perhaps I've been asleep all this time,
Not awoken by the time racing by,
But somehow, I think I missed it,
Somewhere, somehow, some place,
I lost the innocence in my eyes,
The softness in my cheeks,
The tiny fingers curled around my parents,
My small body smothered by teddy bears,
My hello kitty duvet covers and pillows,
The Peppa pig pyjamas,
The barbie dolls at every corner of the house,
The princess dresses scattered across my floor,
And scooter cuts, bike bruises,
When was the last time I asked
For a made-up bedtime story
Or for my mum to brush my hair,
To walk me to school every day.
But now as each day goes by,
Fizzy drinks become vodka,
Bikes become cars,
Scooters become motorbikes,
Kisses on the cheek turn into sex,
Getting high no longer means
swinging in the playground,
Protection doesn't mean
Wearing a helmet anymore,
Remember when your dads' shoulders
Were the highest place on earth,
And mum was superwoman?
The only enemies you ever had
Were you siblings in a nerf gun fight,
The worst pain you felt was scraping your knees,
Cough medicine was the only drug you knew,
Wearing a skirt didn't make you a slut,
And appearances meant nothing.
The only goodbyes meant waiting until tomorrow?
...

Leia Lous

...

Yet we said we couldn't wait to grow up.
When was the last time I lacked a care in the world?
I don't quite know where you draw the line
Between childhood and not,
But all I know is that I've never been
less excited for a birthday.

~*I hate birthdays*

anger.

Tonight, we sat in your car,
And I told you how much I hurt,
How much I cry,
How much I feel,
How much I carry,
How much I die inside.

Then I told you how much I try,
And you told me it's not good enough.

Snap out of it you said,
Get over it you said,
You only want attention you said,
Just stop for God's sake you said.

Tonight, we sat in your car,
And I gave up.

~Conversations at the steering wheel

Leia Lous

Your anger is the part of you
that knows your mistreatment,
Your heartbreak, and your fear,
are unacceptable and unfair.
Your anger knows you deserve
Better and to be treated with kindness,
For you deserve the kind of love
You give to everyone else,
Your anger is a part of you
that loves you and understands.
But you can't fight fire with fire.
The trouble with anger is,
it grabs you by the neck
And refuses to let go of you.
You are no longer in control
of yourself anymore, anger is.
You see, when anger is the boss,
you get unintended consequences,
From your unintended actions,
For you can no longer think straight
Now that you have lost yourself
To the fire.

~Lost to the fire

Leia Lous

Anger is sadness in fight-mode.
Anger will cost you far more than it earns.
Anger is something you wish didn't stick around,
But anger somehow always returns.
Anger is the bodyguard of sadness,
they say the only real way out is vulnerability,
For where there is anger there is always pain,
Underneath is a sensitivity.
Anger is a punishment that we give to ourselves
for someone else's mistakes,
Our heart chooses to rebel,
unaware that it could break.
So, when anger next gives you a visit,
When it creeps into your blood until it boils,
Remember you are stronger than a surge of rage,
As well as an ocean of tears that will sink into your soil.
So, avoid the anger, and try not to cry,
Just say fuck you
and hit them with goodbye.

~Hit them with goodbye

I want to hurt you
The way you hurt me.

I want to rip your heart
Into a thousand pieces,
And scatter them across
Your bedroom floor.

I want to make you cry
So much that you struggle
To even breathe
sleep is no longer an option.

I want to watch you fall apart
Bit by bit until there is
Nothing left of you to love
And nothing left worth living.

But instead, I take it out on
Everyone I love,
I'll have to apologise later.
I take it out on
My bedroom wall,
That I'll have to cover
with a picture frame.
I take it out on
my own body,
Now I should see a doctor for that.

I hold so much anger and resentment,
To someone I still can't help but
Love with all my heart.
I destroyed myself,
Just for you to turn around
And laugh at me.

~Hurt you, hurt m

Leia Lous

What good is sorry?
When what you apologise for,
Has already cut deep enough to scar.
What good is sorry?
When the words you spilt out,
Has already sunk into my fragile skin.
What good is sorry?
When the look you just gave me,
Has crawled its way from my eye to my heart.
What good is sorry?
When your words don't mean anything to me anymore.
What good is sorry?
When you never even meant it.

~Sorry is just a word

Leia Lous

I understood
That you did not know
How to love me,
And I would have been
okay with that,
If you'd have just
Felt the need to try.
What I never understood
Was how you thought
I would be okay,
With you force feeding me
The guilt
That you could taste
In your own mouth.
Now I have
regurgitated that guilt,
Onto a plate with
Your name on it,
Because I'm getting
Pretty sick
Of how sorry sounds,
Coming straight
Out of your mouth.
I am not okay
Because
It's not okay
For you to make
Me feel like this.
Now it's your turn to
Try
To
understand.

~*It's not ok*

How can you say you love me,
When you've only seen my skin,
And not the thirsty seeds I hide,
That grow deep within,
You've not been here long enough,
To encourage more living to start,
Or find the run-down sandcastle,
That's built inside my heart,
Don't mark me with your footprints,
If you plan to leave too soon,
And only want to know me,
When my flowers are already in bloom,
Because my garden of roses might be pretty,
But it's not all for you the beauty that it brings,
And if you think my winter is too cold,
You do not deserve my spring,
For if you are not here to love me,
For every change in season inside and around,
Then you cannot love me at all,
I am the wrong flower you have found.
For I can't promise you rainbows,
If the clouds begin to weep,
I can't promise to be the sunflower,
That never goes to sleep,
I can't be a tree smothered in blossom,
If along comes winter to make it snow,
If you don't want me when I'm bare and empty,
Just leave with the wind and go,
Don't you dare pull or twist or cut,
At my delicate roots below.

~Don't deserve my spring

Leia Lous

I wish I could put my foot on the break,
Because it's making me carsick.
I am changing way too fast,
No one told me it was this exhausting.
You told me it looks as though
I've just been speeding through hell,
But going through hell was no match
To the thought that you could tell.
It makes me angry that I'll be dead,
Before I ever admit that I am scared.
Scared of the paralysing feeling
That the truth may be
I am going nowhere.
It's like the car has broken down,
And everyone else is aware.
Its causing a build-up of traffic,
Everyone screaming at me
to put my foot down
And get the hell out of there.

~*Carsick*

Leia Lous

There is a scream waiting
At the bottom of my stomach,
that forces its way to my mouth,
As if there was a demon living
Within me of whom id never met before.
All I can feel since is pure anger,
I don't want anyone close to me,
Anyone to touch me,
Or talk to me.
I feel an urgent need to isolate
Myself from every single person.
It'll be safer, easier to choose not to stay,
Because I'm not convinced that
I can bear any more pain or heartache,
I will simply self-destruct in flames.
I know I'm hiding the truth even from myself,
of how much this is really to do with sadness
and the scars that just won't heal,
Rather than to do with anyone
Who is only trying to help me.
Yet these fists clench and my teeth lock up,
When someone's mouth spits out the words

'Are you okay?'
NO WHY CAN'T YOU SEE.
'I'm fine thanks.'

~I'm fine thanks

Leia Lous   71

I don't really pay much attention,
To the news of the world ending,
Simply because the world,
It has ended for me many times,
And began again the next morning.
I suppose it's like the boy that cried wolf,
So many times, I thought
My world was ending,
But it ended up being yet another beginning,
Maybe one day,
I'll think my world is ending,
And simply ignore it because of
The exhaustion of trying to stay alive for it,
Turns out this time my world really will end,
What would I have lived for?
Will I feel relief that this time it really is over?
Happy I won't have to wake up and
Go through it all again?
Or will I feel my blood boil inside,
So infuriated with myself,
That I had not treated the life I had been given,
The way it deserved,
With love and kindness,
Not anger and hate.
For I thought there was no point in living,
If my world had theoretically already ended,
But if I had realised that life still goes on,
Maybe I wouldn't be so afraid of living,
After all the people who left me had gone.

~The end of the worl

Leia Lous   72

I used to feel like a glow stick,
There to entertain,
To lighten up people's faces,
Happiness was my domain.
I would brighten up someone's day,
A smile would never leave my face,
Sometimes it felt like a duty,
Like if I frowned it would be a disgrace.
I was a walking and talking
little miss sunshine,
I was everyone source of medicine,
I felt my life was no longer mine.
When I was young, I thrived as her,
being a glow stick felt great,
Until the other emotions pushed to the side,
Became a massive weight.
As I grew older it made me want to hide,
Like feeling sad would be a crime,
I thought no one would want me,
Ended up losing so many people in time.
When I was at my lowest,
when others took not what I could afford to give,
but all that I was and all that I had,
Draining the life out of me like I was a sieve.
When my love and passion began to fail
because they took so much out of me
in a scheming and manipulative way,
anger somehow saved me,
Some of the pain started to go away.
I needed to get the pain out of me,
I got angry enough to save myself,
Angry enough to scream out the truth and
Remove those people that in the back of my mind
sat on a shelf.
A bit of righteous anger,
and righteously deserved,
in the right moment, in the right situation,
can be a good thing, for the truth must be heard.
...

Leia Lous

...

Friends are either radiators or drains,
If they are radiators they will warm you inside,
If they are drains, they will steal from you,
Take out the life you have left til you die.
From the outside looking in,
I bet it looks all happy and bright,
Being a glow stick, being little miss sunshine,
But you don't see how they use and abuse my light.
People take my kindness for a weakness,
And treat me however they like,
Thinking I would never react with anything
other than a smile,
But my mind is so angry it's gone on strike.
My mum tells me 'You must pick your battles',
Well, I'm full of rage and I've picked them all,
Because me, the sun, I've exploded, I'm a forest fire,
I refuse to let them make me feel so small.
How dare you make me feel like
I'm not allowed to be angry or sad,
I am only one human just like you,
But if you live in darkness and prefer to
steal other people's sun,
How on earth could you understand?

~righteous anger, righteously deserve

When I was just a child,
I feared the monsters under my bed.
They had red beady eyes,
With a murderous look,
Their mouths dripping with blood,
Reading my terror like a book.
Blades and daggers for teeth,
Like they'd slice me in half,
A voice like a revving engine,
Watching me tremble they'd laugh.
They shifted at a lion's pace,
Like if I sprinted it would be no help,
Because they had six legs, four arms,
They would devour me swifter than a yelp.
Now I've grown up,
I know they were never real.
The monsters were never under my bed,
They lived rent free in my head.
They have soft brown eyes,
With a kindness in their look,
Their mouths lined with lipstick,
In their gentle hands a book.
Their teeth white and shiny,
They smile bright and bold,
A voice like a comforting melody,
Their heart built from gold.
They felt the rush of wind through their hair,
They danced lightly in the breeze,
They had two legs, two arms,
They ran freely through the trees.
This monsters in disguise,
It eats at me through the night,
Treats me like a rag doll left on the floor,
Spits on me in spite.
When I was just a child,
I feared the monsters under my bed.
Now I'm no longer a child,
I realise the monster is
Me instead.

~Monsters under my bed

Leia Lous   75

It has somehow occurred to me
That I am a walking paradox,
I want nothing but happiness,
Yet I dwell on things that make me sad,
I have so many dreams to fulfil,
Yet I struggle to get out of my bed,
I crave attention from those who love me,
Yet I reject it when they get too close,
I always say I don't care to your face,
But inside I know I really do,
I almost hate myself,
But I also love who I am,
I always feel so insecure,
But I know the poets would adore me,
I am a walking paradox and a
Breathing conflicted contradiction,
The frustrating part is,
If I can't even figure myself out,
How is anyone else meant to?

~Walking parado

Leia Lous

Sometimes,
I'm not even sure if I'm sad
Or just overwhelmingly angry.
I must hold back my fury
And disguise it with tears.
What I really want to do,
Is shout, scream, kick off,
But all I seem to do is cry.
It's like I've been so petrified
Of a raised voice
And a raised fist,
That I forgot how to defend myself.
I end up so overcome with
Sadness,
That my anger just sits back
And watches.
Yet it seems to make me
Even more angry,
Do I not deserve the value?
Of the searing hot red feeling,
Fire is cleansing
It disinfects,
I want to be rid of the
Pent up rot
Inside my mind.

~disinfectant

Leia Lous

I constantly ask the world,
Why can't I be like the sky?
How she ignites her fire and shines,
Every
Single
Day.

How she never gives up on her glow,
No matter how many clouds
Try to dim her light,
She still finds a way to shower the world
In her beauty,
Even through the cracks of the shadows.

How she can come together with the
Sorrow of the rain,
Like a flickering flame of an old love affair,
And turn the worst of a storm,
Into something so beautiful.
The colourful array of a rainbow.

The suffering silence after the rainfall,
How quickly the sky pulls herself back together.
Oh, to be her.

~Oh, to be the sk

Leia Lous

The Rising.

recovery.

Depression is silent
You never hear it coming,
And then suddenly,
On a random Monday,
It's the loudest voice
In your head.

It's no longer silent
When you are on the floor crying,
And there you've been for days.
In the minds of all those around,
That is a sign of weakness.
But-

That is you being strong,
That is you trying your hardest,
To get through the pain and the hurt
As best you know how.
So let it out, release.

No one else can decide
What your strong looks like,
After all you are gifting your tears
Some freedom for themselves.

~Depression is silent

Leia Lous

Sometimes,
It feels like I am
Hitting a wall,
Like I fell forward,
Or drove too fast,
Or ran to a dead end,
And met with the wall.
The wall that
Reflected me,
Or at least how others
Can see me.
The wall was blank,
Perfectly empty,
With an unbreakable
Protection.
I am built with the same
Vigorous structure,
In hope no harm
Could be done to me.
So, I approached this wall,
And the feeling that I'm
hitting it,
When I took a second look,
It softly reminded me,
That walls aren't built to break,
Or to crash into,
Or stop you in your path,
Sometimes walls are there
For you to lean and rest on.
So, I stood with my back
against the wall,
And I stopped to catch my breath,
Before carrying on
With my journey.

~Walls aren't built to brea.

Leia Lous

Sometimes I think I am like a vinyl
Spinning round on a record player,
I sound like a beautiful calming melody,
Or a soulful blues rhythm,
Or maybe I'm a hardcore rock n roll tune,
Or a light and simple ballad reflecting
A sentimental and romantic character.
But, you see this vinyl,
Its bears quite a few scratches,
From how many times it has been
used and abused,
So, as it plays its music,
It can skip, jump, slow down or fasten up,
It doesn't sound so perfect anymore,
But this vinyl still plays, right until the end.

~I am like a vinyl

Leia Lous

I guess I don't hate my scars,
I don't love them,
But maybe they love me.
They have stayed with me
Longer than most people have.
They try to tell me everyday
That maybe I inflicted pain
On myself,
But I am still here to see them.
And that is almost like
A symbol of hope,
A ladder going upwards,
Finding my way out.
But then I remember
That someday they will fade,
Leave me like everyone else.
But maybe that's okay.
Their departure means
I can lift my arms to fly again,
I have climbed that ladder,
I'm standing on my own two feet
Stronger than when I was
at the bottom.
I don't hate my scars,
I don't love them,
They taught me lesson
That nothing is permanent.
One day,
I will be okay
Without needing scars
to remind me I am still here.
Ill kiss them goodbye
As they leave.

~Ladder

Leia Lous

To heal a wound
You must stop touching it,
You must let it breathe,
Allow it to heal at its own pace.
Treat it with kindness,
And the kind of care it requires,
Maybe that's a long walk,
Or a hot relaxing bath,
Or blasting your favourite song,
Or hugging your loved ones,
Or opening up to a stranger,
Or finding a routine that
Allows you the time to focus on you
And what brings you happiness,
Feelings are temporary,
And they can be changed.
Create your own first aid box,
Filled with the things that
Help you recover from the pain
You are feeling.
Scratches disappear,
Grazes scab up,
Cuts stop bleeding and scar,
Scars fade,
Frowns will turn upside down,
You will be smiling once again.

~First aid box

Leia Lous

What I need is to hear the sounds
Of the ocean
As I lie in bed
Alone
with my thoughts
Just to remind me
That there are
Bigger
Things
out there than
What I am feeling
Right now.
My bed will never be big enough to devour me.

What I need is to touch my ear to a seashell
To hear the escape
As I lie here
Trapped
By my thoughts
Just to remind me
That there will
Always
Be
A way to
Peace.
Even in the smallest of places.

What I need is to feel the rain
Run down my cheeks
As I lie in bed
Dead
Inside my thoughts
Just to remind me
That I am still
Alive
Feeling
The touch of cold and bitter
But the touch I can feel.
The sky can cry for me, it helps me like that.

~What I need as I lie in b

Leia Lous   86

A common misconception,
That I wish people were not told,
Is that the medicine to cure
Negativity,
Is positivity.
What if the anecdote we really need,
Is some warmth and comfort.
To accept that this negativity,
Is how I am feeling now,
But alter the way we respond to that.
Positivity only hugs you in the words
That there is no reason for you
To feel this way,
The sun is shining.
Warmth asks you
to play your favourite song,
To go sit and gaze at the stars,
To go eat some chocolate,
To go watch your comfort movie.
Sometimes,
Warmth lays and cuddles you
Reminding you to simply
Just breathe for a few moments.
Positivity can only heal
Those who are in a state where
Recovery seems a few steps away,
Warmth can heal
those who lack the strength
Needed to be positive,
But are wrapped in the gentle
Process of recovery.
Breathing through the baby steps.

~Warmth is the anecdote

Leia Lous

You must realise that
You are still here,
No matter how gone you may feel.
Under all the messy things,
The piles of clothes on your floor,
Under the bottles filled with tears,
And the scribbled pages of sorrow,
Under the stress,
the anxiety,
the sadness,
the anger,
You are still you,
You just have to dig deep
To find yourself again.
Come up for some air,
It's a clearer mind up here,
You must pull yourself up,
Let go of all that weight,
So you can stand on two feet
And regain that strength
To pick up the pieces
and clean up the mess
As best you can yourself,
For if you cannot rely on those
Who claim to love you,
Then you must rely on
Yourself.
You are the only one
That will go through everything
And remain by your side
With yourself
No matter what.

~*Under the mes*

Leia Lous

Sometimes I wish
People wouldn't always say
Have a good day,
When I know full well,
It won't be good days
For a very long time.
I want them to tell me
Have a day, just a day,
Be alive for that day,
Breathe through that day,
Whether it be good or bad,
You survived it,
That's enough to be proud of,
When living seems so hard.
Make sure to eat something,
Wear whatever feels comfortable,
Just relax and do your thing,
Practice what makes you feel like
You deserve this life,
And this life is yours to live.
That's all I want to hear,
When the clouds come to visit,
And the sun is sleeping.
Today is still a day
An opportunity to live,
Whether the sun is shining
Or not.

~Clouds come to visit

Leia Lous

I think its brave
That you choose to wake up,
Even when sleeping is the easiest way
to escape from everything.

I think its brave
That you get up every day,
Even if your bones ache and your mind need
Nothing but rest.

I think its brave
That you try so hard all the time,
Because you believe things can and will get better,
even when you feel like simply giving up.

I think its brave
That you keep going,
Even when life is giving you so many reasons
To stop.

I think it's so brave,
That you choose to walk through hell,
Just to come out the other side
Bearing wings.

~I think it's so brav

Leia Lous

It happens at home,
It happens on the bus,
It happens within five minutes of school,
After ten minutes,
An hour,
Five hours,
It happens around friends,
It happens around family,
It happens when I'm not alone,
Even more so when I am alone.

It happens when I'm eating,
It happens when I'm drinking,
It happens when I'm getting dressed,
It happens when I'm walking,
When I'm talking,
When I'm listening,
When I'm thinking,
It happens always.

Except-
Except when I'm writing,
When it's just me, my pen and my notebook,
Alone with my thoughts, escaping,
Running wild in stampedes across the page,
Drawing pictures in form of poetry,
It doesn't happen when I write,
And write,
And write,
And write.

All the things I wish I could say out loud,
Scream, shout, cry, whisper.
But at least between the hardback leather,
And the freedom of lines on pages,

...

Leia Lous

I know that my thoughts,
I know that my feelings,
My sadness,
My anger,
My heartbreak,
My grief,
My love,
My happiness,
My growth,
My recovery-
I know that I am safe.

~Depression vs a noteboo

Some people have described me
As a perfectionist,
But I'm not sure that's the case.
You see the thing is,
As humans,
Occasionally the actions we take,
The words we spill out,
The way we look from day to day,
Is not always for ourselves.
We think so much about how
Those around us will see us,
The impression we are giving,
What their opinions would be.
For what, I wonder?
Until last night, and I realised
I am guilty as charged for caring.
I have scribbled down an ocean
Of my own poetry,
Usually written at 3am in the dark,
Or a random Monday morning blues time.
Whenever the moon reminds me of someone,
And it's always the same person,
If you know what I mean.
When the wind whispers a word to me,
When the rain triggers a feeling.
Sometimes it's even when I am just
Staring blankly at a flickering candle,
I forget that one day we will burn out too,
So, I write, and I write,
I write so my tears are on a page -
Probably crumpled in a draw.
I write so my smiles are on a page -
Probably neat in a book.
I write so my laughs are on a page -
Probably so I can find it one day and giggle.
I write so my heart is on a page -
Probably hidden so no one can harm it again.
Some people have described me
As a perfectionist,
But I'm not sure that's the case.

...

Leia Lous

...

Maybe I do have mountains of poems
That's I could share with you today,
Maybe I chose not to read them,
Even after all the hours of writing they took,
Maybe that's because
Those poems are me.
Those poems are my life.
Those poems are everything I feel,
Everything I see,
Everything I think,
Everything that has happened in this life of mine.
Maybe I am a bit frightened,
Intimidated at the thought you could know those things,
Read through those moments I am alone with pen and paper.
If I were a perfectionist,
I would make everything perfect.
I can guarantee you that this notebook here,
Teardrops, lipstick stains, tears and rips,
Probably little pieces of my heart too,
And definitely coffee.
No one is perfect, no life is perfect, no poem either.
I write from my heart and my soul,
Battered and bruised, but plasters too.
At the end of the day, what is it for?
Constantly stressing about
what others think of us,
What others see in us,
What others say about us.
Perfection is overrated,
I'd rather have a few scars,
many bad hair days,
One morning waking up looking like a witch,
But the next day maybe a princess.
I'd rather be perfectly imperfect,
At least I have a story to tell,
And poems to write.
One day, ill shout them from the rooftops.

~Perfection is overrate

Leia Lous

94

I feel so out of character.

It's like I'm somewhat in denial,
I'm grieving the happiness
They say I felt as a child.
I thought it felt like walking on air,
Like jumping on clouds,
Like dancing in the breeze.

But those cliche ideas,
Though they were gentle thoughts
For my wounded mind,
Were only fantasy stories
For mothers and fathers,
to wrap their children in cotton wool.

They were stories
that stay with the young,
Only words on a page,
But those words prick at your heart
When the blue skies and sunshine
Don't always show up.

Like the story is neglecting you,
You don't deserve that life,
But the stories are wrong.
After all, that's life.

You can't always be the princess
With dolled up hair
And the perfect smile
When everyone looks in awe
and forever stares.
You can't always be that prince
With the charming manner,
And the strong build,
When everyone relies on you
but never cares.

...

Leia Lous

95

...

A Plaster cannot fix the heart.
A fairy tale book cannot tell the story of real life.
You are not a princess; you are not a prince.
You are a girl; you are a boy.
Don't let the old tell you how to think.

I am not entitled to all the happiness in world,
And that is okay.
I am not punished with all the sadness in the world,
It's not here to stay.
In life you will find a balance
A weight and a release.
One that will teach you a lesson,
More than Snow White
and the seven dwarfs
Ever will.

~ out of characte

Leia Lous

'Proud'.
Not a common word I use to describe me.
Not something I would ever say out loud.
Not something others seem to whisper in my ear either.

'I am proud of myself' - never said, never thought.
'I am proud of you' - maybe said, maybe thought.
But never heard.

'Proud' is a word I feel neglected by,
Like it's not there, non-existent.

Or maybe others see me as not worthy of 'proud'?
Maybe I see myself as not worthy of 'proud'?

My notebook,
All the torn pages,
All the ones damp by tears,
All the ones crumpled by anger,
All the ones ripped with heartbreak,
All the ones fresh with happiness,
All the ones empty, waiting for change.

My notebook would disagree.

If I am still living and breathing,
After all the pain,
the sadness, anger, grief, heartbreak, love, happiness, growth, recovery.

If I am still living and breathing,
enough to write another poem,
I should be-

'Proud'.

~A simple word

Leia Lous

growth.

Like a petal will fall,
Like the leaves will weep,
Like the branches will snap,
Reminder this all repeats.

Like my heartache is throbbing,
Like my eyes will cry,
Like the mascara shall run,
Reminder my tears will dry.

Though all this feels endless,
And the cycle breeds pain,
A new petal, leaf, branch shall grow,
A mended heart you shall have again.

~Mother Nature

Be patient with yourself,
Healing takes time,
Healing implies kindness,
Taking care of yourself is not a crime.
Healing means changes,
Healing could mean starting over,
You shouldn't apologise for healing,
If it is giving you closure.
After healing then comes becoming,
And becoming is far from easy,
For when things change inside you,
Things change around you; you see.
Be patient with yourself,
For you are gardening your soul,
Some flowers are meant to bloom quicker than others,
Some things are simply out of your control.
The strongest of flowers,
They choose to bleed in silence,
Have no one to applaud their growth,
Since there was no one to give them guidance.
These flowers had no one watching
their difficult healing process,
They bloomed by themselves in silence,
Learnt to be proud of their own progress.
So, just know that when you have been
covered from head to toe in darkness,
You have been planted,
Whether you reach for the light or not,
you will grow and you will bloom regardless.

~Strongest of flowers

A flower does not think of competing
with the flower that sits next to it,
it just blooms in its own beautiful way,
As best as it sees fit.
The flowers became a dancing rainbow,
as if light and music had found a new way
to blossom together in harmony,
And each show their own beauty each day.
Though you shouldn't try to force
a new bud to open faster,
to see the beauty you know is inside,
For a fragile stem cannot be fixed with a plaster.
But nature has its way,
its own timing, its own pace,
and perhaps this flower wasn't ready yet,
Wasn't strong enough to show her face.
A shower in-between the warmth,
And a few more sunny days,
and maybe it would be ready to bloom,
she just had to wait, for those shining rays.
she became a tall and proud sunflower,
Turning her back to the darkness,
Following the sun,
For deep down she knew that now she had bloomed,
Her life had only just begun.

~Proud sunflower

I fell in love with the ocean,
Because it made me realise
How small I am
In such a big world,
The vastness of the body of water
And then the body of me,
It simply doesn't compare.
It grounded me,
Made me realise I am only one life
Of millions more,
So why should I try to be
Anyone but who I am,
No two of the 7 billion people
That live on this planet are the same,
2 million species live in the ocean,
All of them different to each other,
Yet they too share the same home,
The ocean.
A goldfish could try to be a blue whale,
But really it can only be a goldfish,
And I can only be me,
The ocean taught me that
Being myself will always be
More than enough.

~The ocean taught m

Leia Lous

Growth is so easily misunderstood,
Why everyone seems to believe
Growing only limits itself
To growing upwards and forwards,
I will never know.
Sometimes growth means
Backwards and downwards.
Coleus plants hang low,
Yet they dress in red velvet
With silver linings,
With a name meaning
'Red trailing queen'.
Nasturtium plants dangle down,
With pad-like leaves and
Beautiful bright flowers.
Ferns swing below,
Surfing in the air with
Their foliage attractions.
Silver falls plants trail beneath,
With unique leaves
That develop rapidly.
They are still growing and blooming,
In the same way that
trees, bluebells, clematis, honeysuckle do,
Upwards or downwards, you grow.
Just because you feel low
And as down as down could be,
Growth is ever lasting,
Why stop there?
After all,
sunflowers face away from the sun
Before they bloom and stare
At the healing rays of light.

~Red trailing queen

Autumn understands depression,
Like it's a three-month therapy session,
For the hurting souls that
dread the cold and lonely of winter.
Autumn shows us how leaves fall
And lose touch of the life
within them.
So perhaps it's inevitable that
people too can plummet to rock bottom,
And lose grip of the tears
Running down their faces.
But what those tears fail to tell you,
Is that when they fall to the ground,
They could become the water needed
For a splash of life to sprout,
To bloom into something magnificent.
The shattered remains of your heart
Left lifeless on the ground,
Could be fresh new seeds to
Create a sense of hopefulness.
Depression can take life from you,
Autumn can teach you what life is.
That you may not be growing,
How you had first imagined as an
Innocent, happy, carefree child,
Diving into the piles of red and orange
Scattered leaves, not ever realising
That those leaves were robbed
Of their lives.
But although life is treating you
Differently to how you expected,
Being a part of all that revives and blooms
all around you darling,
That is a more than good enough reason,
To believe you can regrow and bloom too.

~ Autumn knows depression like it grows on tr

The seasons come as a favourite bedtime story,
each time the same as last time,
and yet different in some compelling way.

Springtime arrives as the first verse of a new song,
never waiting for a lyric upon the perfect ice-free day,
yet tips forward at first chance for the warming light of day.
The newly born sense of light and hope blooms in me.

Summertime arrives tenderly so I could close my eyes
and feel that the meadow and floral blooms
were as much within me as they were around me,
supporting my body upon the warm earth.

Autumn time arrives with slow grace and a steady ease. Though the first
leaves have stumbled to the hydrated soil, though I'm anticipating the
garlands of reds and golds,
The grief felt through the trees remind me
That I must be as patient as she.

Wintertime arrives as an icy serenade to bring out
the warmth within us, with a calmness within the winds spreading as
eddying swirls of light with steadiness,
a bitter yet comforting reminder to move on with the breeze.

Each reminder the same as last time,
And yet I feel differently every time.
As the seasons fly past my bedroom window,
Just as the temperatures change, so do I.

~Just as the temperatures change

Leia Lous

For once in my life,
I don't care if I'm being selfish.
For once in my life,
I'm going to prioritise myself
Over anyone who stands in my path.
For once in my life,
I'm going to make myself happy
Before I put smiles on other people's faces.
For once in my life,
I'm going to make room for myself, my heart and my soul
Before I give my spaces to everyone else.
For once in my life,
I'm going to bloom beautifully on my own
Without needing people to water me.
For once in my life,
It's me
Who comes
First.
I'm going to get better for me,
Before I get better for everyone else.

~Self-growth isn't selfis

Leia Lous

If the presence of courage
isn't due to the absence of fear
but doing what's necessary regardless,
maybe the presence of confidence
isn't due to the absence of insecurity
but knowing you are good enough despite it.
If this may be the case,
maybe the presence of a good nature
isn't due to the absence of intrusive thoughts,
but the conscious choice to act
the way your heart tells you right.
If the presence of growth
Isn't due to the absence of dying
But thriving in what life you have left,
Maybe the presence of happiness
Isn't due to the absence of sadness
But knowing tomorrow is a new day.

~The presence of happiness

This girl spends her time,
Staring at the birds and butterfly
That pounce and dive outside her window,
Envious they were granted the freedom to thrive.
Her arms reached out as she
Gazes longingly up at the sky,
Wishing for the wings
That could teach her to fly,
For she's trapped on earth here,
Her two feet glued to the ground,
The forces of gravity,
Are forever pulling her down,
She wants to be an angel,
But she's only a girl,
Why should she be so different,
To all the others in the world,
And though she's life's puppet,
One day she will break all the strings,
But for now, she's just dreaming,
Of earning her wings.
When that day comes,
And she's grown to soar so high,
She'll befriend the birds and the bees,
For now, she's become the butterfly.
She has been stuck in a cocoon,
For far too long,
But now she's grown wings
Both beautiful and strong,
Now, she's more than ready,
To prove them all wrong.

~Only a girl

Leia Lous

Something that I had to learn,
To finally accept me for me,
Was that on the way to
Finding the raw, honest, true you,
You must understand that
It could also mean the death of
What you once were,
And how people once saw you,
How they thought you would always be,
You must accept this to fully
Be yourself, comfortably.
A butterfly does not wish to be
Trapped inside its cocoon forever,
Its desire is to open its fresh, new wings,
And fly.

~Honest butterfly

Sometimes
I really wish,
That when you looked at someone
They had pictures of all that
Lives in their minds,
Painted all over their body.
I wonder if
Your view would alter,
When you see the bright smiling
People you think you know,
Plastered in colours of black and blue.
Maybe beneath their delicate skin,
Knives, daggers, swords
Stab recklessly at their worn hearts.
Who would know if
Their tears were replaced with laughs,
Their sadness blanketed in beauty,
Their anxiety caked in hugs.
I imagine,
If we could see underneath
The masks we all wear for protection
Our minds plagued with nothingness,
If we could see the truth,
Maybe everyone would pick up
Soft paintbrushes,
And colour each other in hues
Of the sun, of flowers, of life.
Happiness could be shared,
If you show you true colours,
No matter how black and blue
Or yellow and green
You may be.
Don't look around
and foolishly believe,
Look inside
and understand.

~Paint the tru█

Leia Lous

Eventually the sky will heal,
and the drops pass by evaporating,
Sinking into the blanket of clouds,
And all disappears,
strutting only for brief minutes.

Even as it all disappears,
I can still see the water marks
left alone on my clothes,
And sent in the air is a message,
One I shall never forget.

That maybe I hated the rain, the dampness, the bitterness.

But they were the rainbow that came with it,
The splash of colour
among the dull and draining atmosphere,
Of which my body was surrounded.

So now I would smile and wave at the dark clouds,
And embrace them with the warmth from my own heart.

Until the cloudy days and rain sobered me
with the thought of
You.

~sobered by rain

Leia Lous

The moon taught me
That there is beauty
In the darkness too,
That even when
I don't feel whole
I can still brighten up
The space in the room.
So maybe each day
I could be losing more light,
But the moon still
Shows up every day
And she fights to be seen
That's what makes her so bright.
Although it takes time,
For me to become whole,
The moon takes 30 days
For it to become full
So ill follow in the steps
Of her moonlight
And not give up even when
My gleam is small,
For I ignite and I burn
So that I can be seen
And when the next
Full moon arrives
I will illuminate more vividly
Than I have ever been.

~Full moon

Leia Lous

You always told me,
This too shall pass.
That stuck with me
Like a tattoo across my heart,
Like a scar that doesn't fade,
Like it lived inside my mind.
Reminded me that
Nothing is permanent
And wherever I may be now,
Life is ever-changing
Like the beauty of nature,
And one day it will pass
And I will grow from
Everything that tried to
cut me at the roots,
Because all flowers
Wilt
Heal
Grow
bloom.
Time shall pass,
And one day I'll have a
Garden filled with the most
Beautiful of roses,
daffodils, lilies, daisies.

~For Rachel

Leia Lous

love.

looked up at the sky, a sense of promise, adventure and a feeling I was not yet familiar with filled the air. It was somewhat a bittersweet sensation, warm and comforting but in the back of my mind it was fear that dominated the pulses released from my aching heart in these confusing moments.

They say it's beautiful, falling in love.

say the concept is something that truly twists and turns my brain like the waves that control the ocean through the chaotic storms that occasionally wash over the clear jet blue skies as it transforms to arkness and destruction. I never thought of love as a feeling, more of a concept, a theory, an action that develops into a stronger force, but it always is crushed by the truth.

Vhat truth? Is love something true? Surely if love were the truth, there vould be no false? Be no storms, darkness, destruction. Honesty? Love unpredictable, and terrifying, and incredible... it takes the strongest of earts to understand. That I am never sure I will accomplish. But here I am, falling.

~The act of falling

Leia Lous

She always had that look about her,
That look of divergence,
Of eyes that see things much too far,
Some sights that cause disturbance,
And of thoughts that wander off the
Edge of the world,
They fall right down to her heart
And inside my heart they uncurled,
And a mind that was a far cry from
The normality of others,
She could understand things,
That shouldn't be understood yet,
And due to that she suffers,
They say knowledge is power,
But to her this cannot be true,
For what she knows scares her
Of things she is yet to do.
Like falling in love,
And settling down,
Putting her trust in somebody,
But the idea makes her frown.
For the cruelty of people,
And the reality of life,
Makes her fear the risk of her future,
The unease cuts her like a knife.
For what if her world is turned upside down,
What if it all goes wrong?
These questions running through her head,
What if love doesn't belong?
Because she grew up without love,
Love to her is a stranger,
How could she possibly be for it,
When she thinks it only brings danger,
For love will suffocate her,
She would rely on it like air,
But she deserves love like oxygen,
For a heart like hers is so rare.

~Look of diverge

Leia Lous

I spoke to the moon today,
And I told him of our love,
And how warm and light
You make me feel inside,
Like I have the power
To brighten up people's lives.
Just like the sun does.

It was that moment,
That I realised just how
Important you made me feel,
And to me you were everything.
The moon, the stars, the sun, the earth.
You were all of it.

In front of the moon
and the sky filled with stars,
I confessed my love to you.
The stars glistened brighter than ever,
And then the sun arrived.
The moon left gladly,
Knowing that I was no longer
Living in the darkness.
Because,
you.

~Confession to the moon

Leia Lous

We were so perfect together,
Like how the sun and the moon
Complement each other in their
Daily dose of performing
In front of the overwhelming crowds
Of human life.
I was the sun; you were the moon.
Bathed in the light of the sun,
the moon was more beautiful
than any of the shining stars around.
Overcome with excitement of
passing her one and only moon,
The sun showered her glow brighter
than any of the shining stars around.
The sun and the moon adored
All that was above, beneath, around
Their theatre of abundance,
But more than anything known to life
They adored each other.

~We performed in the sk

Leia Lous

My favourite music
Has always been sad,
For they became the story of my life
When all my days were bad.
My favourite time of day
Has always been night-time,
So, I can finally collapse in bed
Every phone call id hit decline.
So, I find it almost ironic
That I fell in love with you,
The brightest person I have ever met,
It's like you gifted me a whole new view.
I have always loved the moon
And the darkness that surrounds it,
Yet you make me want to love the sun,
Fascinated by all that's in its orbit.
You to me are out of this world,
Both the sun and my moon,
Because you glow all day long,
Ever grateful I met you so soon.
I guess that's why I need you
For I am not lost in the dark,
Or blinded by the lights,
With you by my side
there's always a spark.
So, I'll stop singing sad songs,
And play here comes the sun,
For every time I look in your eyes,
I feel my life has just begun.

~A spark

Leia Lous

119

Falling in love is quite terrifying,
In such a comforting way,
Like this fear will lift you higher
Than the clouds above,
And show you just how much life
You had never seen, felt, touched, tasted
Ever before.
The sky is your arms,
And it wraps every inch of me in clouds.
The clouds were your kisses,
Gently brushing against my skin.
The sunlight was your smile,
It brightened up my cloudiest of days.
The moonlight was your whispers,
Easing me with your words through the night.
The rainfall was your touch,
Each drop like a pinch to remind me I am alive,
Each drop that kissed my body
in those days that you and I were together.
The sky is our love,
Its scale unimaginable, infinite.
As if we could keep soaring higher and higher,
And never meet the finish line.

~*The sky is our lov*

Leia Lous

You were like the sea.
A bit of chaos,
A bit of calm,
But always comforting
To be around.
I loved the sea.
I would always find myself
Down by the water,
Unable to resist the urge,
To run my feet through the
gentle wash on the sand.
To feel what the sea was like.
The sea seems so simplistic
When you stare at it,
Just a huge pool of water
With waves and storms.
But you look beneath
the surface,
And the sea
becomes a stranger,
Someone you've never seen before.
The sea hides away
The magical parts
That make it so special.
Beneath the surface,
A whole new sense
of life,
of colour,
of adventure,
And of beauty,
Stays hidden from those
Resting on its shore.
The real life of the sea
Is too vulnerable
For those above to abuse.
Maybe that's what made
Me and you
So special

...

Leia Lous

...
Because you let me
Swim with those fish
dance on the coral
Twist through waves
And dive into the truth
Of the sea, the truth of you.
I saw parts of you no one had before,
And you were everything
Anyone could dream of.
You don't just remind me of the sea,
You remind me of the depths
And the unknown of what life can be,
If you just dare to try.

~Beneath the surfa

I hated my eye colour,
Saw it as nothing but a dull and dirty brown,
I wished for the adventurous deep blue of an ocean,
Where admirers' hearts would drown in the fascination,
He told me it hurt him when he realised,
That I see it so differently to the likes of his own eyes,
He tells me of the way my eyes are a story,
That he wants to read his way through to the final line,
He tells me how they hold specks of stolen sunlight,
That warms him inside when he gazes,
And how they hold a depth of raw emotion,
That every time paralyses him into a trance,
He tells me they're a mixture of melted chocolate,
Perfect for when he is craving something sweet,
But he tells me they grasp a stare that's so unfaltering,
That he struggles to meet me eye to eye,
As if he is falling right down the rabbit hole,
When he looks into my dull and dirty brown eyes,
He tells me the brown of my eyes reflect
earths free and everlasting beauty and growth,
That he yearns to memorise and live in always,
He tells me that when he was exhausted from not belonging,
My eyes, they made him feel like he had been found,
Like he was at home in the forest within my eyes,
He could run like the wind through the autumn trees,
Showered in colours of sunsets,
Feeling the comforting warmth of the sunlight,
Stolen only to accompany his own heart.
So, he tells me, as he gazes into these eyes of mine,
That he only wishes that I never say again,
That my eyes are simply just brown,
For some eyes can touch you more
Than hands every could.

~Brown eyed girl

Leia Lous

You remind me so much of autumn,
The way it arrives with a buoyant lack of subtleness,
Colours of brown that provide a comforting quilt to earth,
Yet everything else around avalanches
In colours of volcanoes and fireworks and festivals.
Like nature is cheering for the summer trees to rain us
In giant confetti of falling leaves along the sidewalk.
Autumn makes the trees giggle and let their hair down,
Dress appropriately for the coming season,
In the most vibrant of hues stood with a humble boldness.
Autumn makes me want to soak my eyes in the scarlet aura,
And dance on the golden and red carpets resting on paths.
Autumn has a freshly calm air about it
with a hint of an earthly aroma,
the fragrance of homeliness.
You remind me so much of autumn,
Because you feel like home to me,
Like a staggering tower made of a colourful array
Of those fallen leaves beauty,
For me to dive into a rest my eyes,
As it wraps every inch of my body
Like a blanket on a winter's day.
You feel to me,
Like autumn feels to earth.

~ In every breath the autumn
is in us to

Leia Lous   124

If I were to build a house,
A house that felt like home to me,
Your eyes would be the windows,
For I can see my life in your eyes,
Your smile would be the front door,
For it greets me every time,
Your heart as the fireplace,
For the best form of comfort is your love,
Your arms would hold it together,
For there's no place safer than that,
Your breath to make it warm,
For it is the source of my oxygen.
In this house,
I would fill it with all the love,
All the passion,
All the beauty,
All the happiness I have ever known,
And I would make it ours,
Knowing I had finally found a safe place,
That home was you.

~To build a house

Leia Lous

You noticed
the visible flaws of me
and saw my ugliest of moments,
yet you still
perceived to love me.
Whether or not
that love you truly felt,
I sure felt loved by you.

That I will never forget.

You traced my scars,
Like they were
Strokes of paint
On a canvas.
A body and soul
Of abstract art.

That's what you said.
I was art.
I was beautiful.

~A stroke of pair

Leia Lous

I'll write for you a poem,
So, you can read it from time to time,
A story of what you and I could be,
When I can finally call you mine.
In a new world different to this,
Where we are not trapped by expectations
Of how others wish us to be,
We are free from limitations,
We are perfectly imperfect if only they could see,
The world grieves people like you and me.
For we witness the world in a different way,
We see it not for what it is, but what it could be,
It could be a peaceful and beautiful stay,
It has its flaws for sure, but if only they could see,
We reflect the world, and it reflects you and me.
So why are we so hopefully in love,
With what seems so against us,
The world denies our happy ending,
Like our story turns to nothing but dust.
But we are not fazed by what they choose to say,
So, I'll write this poem so long as you stay,
For what's the point in writing it if you will go way.
So, tell me to write us into forever,
If you let my mind run wild,
For we will run always together,
And imagine the world had smiled.
I'll write for you a poem,
We will read it from time to time,
A story of what you and I have become,
For now, I can call you mine.

~I'll write for you a poem

Leia Lous

127

I love it when you call me,
Just cause you want to
Hear my voice.
It's such a small thing,
But the thought
That you found comfort,
In the sound
that comes from my mouth,
Like I spoke in melodies
Or lullabies,
Like I was a song
You listened to on repeat,
Just to remind you
Everything will be okay.

~ Call me

Leia Lous

Isn't it so beautiful-

How trees breathe
So we can exist,
And we exist
So trees can breathe.

We share the same earth,
And sky,
And all the beauty,
But we give each other,
The life necessary to see it.

That's why
When I look at trees,
It's a little reminder of
You
And
Me.

~The trees breathe for us

Leia Lous

happiness.

Sometimes when I can't sleep,
I stay awake and talk to the moon.
He likes to watch and listen,
To those beneath
the never-ending sky
That he calls home.

Because we are grounded,
With roads to cross,
And paths to follow,
And trees to climb,
And flowers to pick,
And earth to stand on.

The moon rules an abyss,
A great sense of nothingness.
He swims in darkness,
He floats in darkness,
He follows the darkness,
But he thrives in the darkness.
Still, motionless stars for company.

He watches and listens,
Because he craves to be rooted
To a floating rock of fascination.
Unaware that those beneath him,
Like myself,
Crave to be swimming in nothingness,
Like he does.
He watches us in awe
His own eyes see the beauty
Of the lives we have down here.
We watch him in awe
Our own eyes watch him glow
Envious of the attention he gets
Guiding people
When they are surrounded
By darkness.

...

Leia Lous

131

...
It's so ironic how we
Crave nothing but another's life
And they crave nothing but ours
Why can't we be happy with what we have?
Because the moon does not have
The wide scenery of opportunities
That earth and human life provides,
But we on earth do not have the power
To shine on our own for the entirety
Of the world to see.

Sometimes when I can't sleep,
I stay awake and talk to the moon.
Tonight, he told me
To shine I must live
And be grateful of what life I have
On such a beautiful planet.
So, I told him,
That to live he must shine
And be grateful of the
Good he does for those in the dark
Because though alone in the sky
The whole of the world
Appreciates his glow.

~talking to Mr moo.

Leia Lous

At first, I feared the things around me in this place.
This place that I call home,
Not a physical home built with bricks,
Where mums, dads, sisters, brothers live,
The home that is myself,
My body, my heart, my soul.
You see, home isn't built in a day.
It takes strength, perseverance, resilience,
And a whole load of coffee,
To create a space within yourself
Where you feel safety, comfort, security.
If I were to look into myself and find my home,
I would see plant pots erupting with
flowers like a dancing rainbow,
as if light and music had found a new way
to blossom together.
I would feel a refreshing flow of air
from the open windows,
enlivening my resting senses
and relaxing my steady, gentle breath.
Through the window streams light,
the fresh rays of gold that flows in
at the birth of every new day.
I would hear the harmonising birdsong
That became the river of the air,
a flowing music that hydrated my tired heart.
I would watch the candlelight flickering in the dark,
the perfect bridge between
the world of the awake and the world of dreams.
I would reach for the rainbow spines
of a banquet of books upon the shelves,
Each performing the chorus in their loud voices.
At first, I feared the things around me in this place.
This place that I call home.
Now my heart is rooted to the ground,
connected to the eternal freedom
That I have found here.

...

Leia Lous   133

...

The ever-growing knowledge of who I am,
When I'm just being me, alone.
Hidden from the judgements of others,
Free from the social constructs that trap us
Into believing we are and must be a certain way
To be accepted.
Sometimes, we need to be alone,
Not to be lonely,
But to indulge in the time we spend with ourselves,
And learn to feel secure in all that we are,
After all,
The only person who will stay with you forever,
Is you, yourself.

~Look for the home within yourse

Leia Lous

Though your mouth lacks the knowledge,
Of the words I long to hear,
You have my full attention.

Though your brain cannot translate,
The jumbled thoughts in my mind,
You make them seem smaller.

Though your arms cannot shield me,
From what lurks within the darkness,
You make me feel a little safer.

Though your warm embraces on the coldest days,
Cannot be a raincoat in the storm,
You keep the grey clouds from consuming me.

Though you are only one human with one heart,
You are the lighthouse that I search for,
When the darkness in my mind comes to play.

You are the reason-
The only reason,
I believe in light, in safe, in warm, in comfort.
I believe that things will get better.

~Thank you

Leia Lous

You never really know the true impact
you have on those around you,
You never really know how your presence,
Could help with what they are going through.
You never know how much someone needed
that smile you just gave them now,
You never know how much your kindness
Could turn someone's whole day around.
You never know how much someone needed
that long hug or deep talk,
You don't realise that could have been the reason,
They got out of bed and went for a walk.
You never know how much someone needed
To have someone like you by their side,
I hope you know how much they appreciate
Having you as their guide.
Perhaps a stranger needs a bit of love,
For today could be their worst,
So don't wait to be kind,
And don't wait for someone else to be kind first.
Don't wait for better circumstances,
or for someone to simply change,
Just be kind, because you never know just how much
someone could need it,
Maybe they will return the same gesture with a smile in exchange.

~Don't wait to be kind

Leia Lous

A little bird told me,
To find happiness in life,
Is like to catch a butterfly
In the palms of your hands
After a long, draining chase.
To catch a butterfly,
With all its energy and determination,
Is incredibly difficult
With only the grasp of two hands.
But,
Once you've caught it,
You'll find that it isn't blood
That's dripping through your fingers,
But pure beauty and magnificence.
The power of nature yet
Something so small as a butterfly,
Something so small as the power
Of a laugh and a smile.
It will take time, and effort,
But you'll catch it one day
And find your happiness.

~Laughs, smiles and butterflies

Leia Lous

The sun is consistent proof
That every day you should wake up and live,
The sun arrives needing not invitation yet feeling welcome.
The light of the sun is a gift of freedom and confidence,
To anyone who cares to see the world awake.
The sun comes as free-spun laughter to this world,
igniting a jocund glow and the brilliant light
hugs the land as the sun stretches out with golden arms.
An embrace that all living things could never resist,
Reason being that only in the light of the sun
can our most vivid hues sing so loud.
our sun, is ignited to inspire warmth, creation,
And the seeking of the beauty within ourselves.

~Rise and shin

Leia Lous

Let November be November.
Let December be December.
Let yourself just
Feel the November rain on your skin,
Admire the clouds change from white to grey,
Indulge in the early arrival of the moon,
Sense the crumbs of ice fall from the sky.
Winter is a long sleep,
A time of less daytime, more night-time.
Whilst the chills may frost you to a snowman,
It attracts the warmth of a flickering flame,
The comfort of a tumble-dried blanket,
The steaming of a hot chocolate,
And the brewing of a new beginning.

Let August be August.
Let October be October.
Let yourself just
Sympathise with the falling of the leaves,
Get wind of the tingling sensation of their crunch,
Witness the energising earthiness anchoring yet propelling,
Appreciate the harmony of each sunset hue.
Autumn is a melancholy song,
The winding down of sunny memories.
Whilst the fall feels like the world goes to sleep,
Fall is also an orange blanket,
A celebration of colours laced with cosiness,
The beauty of a passing sunset,
And the acceptance of a sad goodbye.

Let June be June.
Let July be July.
Let yourself just
Dance among the summerly spotlights,
Breathe in the hot aromatic air,
Fascinate over the humble seeds' transformation
Shouting loud their graffiti-petaled beauty.
Summer sits upon the hill as a floral wedding hat,
Toasting the blooming relationship of people and life.

...

Leia Lous

...

Whilst the summer dares to expose you to life,
The sun steps forth wrapping us in her balmy rays,
Echoes of summer days take the form of flowers
Immune to winter chills,
And summer comes in her own time,
drifting in on a spring breeze,
Wakening the world with a kindness in her warmth.

Let the seasons be seasons.
The same way life is life.
If days are seconds, minutes, hours,
And years are days, months.
Perhaps seasons are life's clockwork,
The twisting and turning of time in ways
That render the heart and the soul
to greatest clarity.

~Life's clockwo

Leia Lous

I live for that feeling when I step outside,
I feel the stroking of the green grass on my feet,
I hear the peaceful humming of birds in the trees,
I see the sky and all its beauty above my head,
I smell the humidity in the air,
I feel the dancing of the wind through my hair,
I hear the whispers from the gossiping trees,
I see the flowers welcome me with open petals,
I smell the freshness of a brand new day.
A brand new day.
A brand new me.

~a new day

Leia Lous

Roses aren't always red,
and violets aren't exactly blue,
why are we told these things so young,
if in reality they are not true.
Smiles aren't always happy,
and frowns aren't always upset,
people judge too quickly and
our feelings are what they forget.
I can't think of any better
representation of beauty than
someone who is unafraid to be themselves,
Those who can admire someone's beauty
without questioning ourselves.
So, stop comparing your life to others,
For there's no comparison between
the sun and the moon,
they shine when it's their time,
And darling your time is coming soon.

~Roses aren't always re

Leia Lous

Happiness is infectious,
It starts as a tingle in my fingers and toes,
much like the feeling I have when I'm nervous,
but instead of anxiety it's warm and it glows.
I feel it pass through me like a gentle wave in the sea,
washing away the stress and worries of my day
to leave me refreshed and clear inside my head,
Reminding me that peace of mind is here to stay.
As the wave fades, I savour the memory
of its gentle touch, and smooth flow,
I soak myself in the water it provides,
For my roots are growing just below.
Let us live like flowers, wild, beautiful,
and drenched in sunlight,
And when the darkness washes over
Let us still glisten as stars in the night.
I have come to love myself for who I was,
who I am, and who I hope to be,
Who I was washed away with the waves,
Who I am holds the strength of a tree,
Who I hope to be isn't the sun, star, sea, tree, nor flower,
It's to just be happy as nothing but me.

~Infectious

Leia Lous

It's such a bittersweet feeling,
When you read the final page
And meet the back cover.
The end of a perfectly imperfect
Rollercoaster of a story.

But I think that's why life is so precious,
Because you can reread the book
But you can't go back and change the lines,
The story will stay the same.
Which is why-

You should chase that sunset.
Kiss that person.
Eat that cake.
Cry to that movie.
Dance like nobody's watching.
Lay in the rain.
Dress in whatever you want.
Sing as if you actually can.
Laugh as loud as possible.
Smile at everyone walking past.

Ride that rollercoaster.

Cherish the moments with meaning.
No one wants to read a book without
A gripping, page turner plot,
And a happy ending.

Meet the back cover and smile.

~The back of a rollercoast

Leia Lous

What makes you so special to me
Is how you notice when something is wrong,
Before I even say a single word,
Your comforting words calm me like a song.
You always know when I need a hug,
Even if I'm shutting myself away,
You can sense when I want to cry my eyes out,
Even when there's a smile on my face.
I never have to ask you for help,
I know you are always there to guide me,
For you remain by my side forever,
Without you how lost I would be.
You have been the rock in this life of mine,
I would feel so helpless without you,
You are the watering can aiding my growth,
As I blossom into something brand new.
Saying thank you isn't merely enough
To tell you just how grateful I am
That you are here, and I am here,
I'll always be your little girl
Though I no longer fit in a pram.
I know I have grown up and changed,
I hope you are proud of what I've become,
For you are my best friend,
my unpaid therapist,
And my superhero,
But most importantly
You are my mum.

~Joanne

I have such a special nan
We stick together like glue,
No other friend in all the world
Will care for me like you do,
When I feel down and blue,
Listening to nan I will always learn
From all her wise and loving kindness
She asks for nothing in return.
The times I come to see you,
All the precious memories I recall,
Of a person so full of sunshine,
And a smile for one and all.
I just wanted to let you know,
You mean more than the world to me,
Only a heart as sweet as yours,
Would give so unselfishly.
The many things you do for others,
And all the times you have been there,
They touch me deep down inside
knowing how much you truly care.
Even though I don't say it enough,
I appreciate everything that you do,
Blessed is an understatement of how I feel,
To have a nan like you.
You are my sunshine,
That's what you used to always sing to me,
I remember those lines off by heart,
My sunshine you will always be.
One day I will sing that to my children,
And every time I'll think of you,
For the lyrics of that lullaby warm my heart,
Knowing you sung them so true.
When they ask me about who you are,
I'll tell them of the memories we made together,
And how I will love you until the end of time,
For as long as the sun shines
you will stay in my heart
forever.

~Co

Leia Lous

There's a very special woman
That I am very close to,
She showed me what it means
To always shine like the sun,
Even when the clouds are chasing you,
For she will forever say
"I can do this"
Even when her body aches,
"It will be okay"
Even with tears in her eyes,
"I am good enough"
Even if people tell her she isn't,
For she knows that
She is the artist of her own life,
She will not give away
The paintbrush to anyone else.
You simply can't say that
Your life is yours
If you are always caring
About what others think,
And letting them control
How your life will be.
It is your life,
And you only have one,
So, she says to me,
"Honestly darling,
As long as you are happy,
Who the hell cares."

~Melanie

I want you to quickly turn back to the first poem in the sadness section in this book and read it. Now, this book was a journey of finding your way out of the darkness and back to the light. Once you have read the first poem flick back and read below... this is how my mindset has changed throughout this journey of my own.

(Now read the first poem, page 8)

...

Sometimes it is okay to be a glow stick,
sometimes we need to break
before we can truly shine.

Printed in Great Britain
by Amazon